Elections and Voting

What's That Got To Do With Me?

Elections and Voting

Antony Lishak

FRANKLIN WATTS
LONDON•SYDNEY

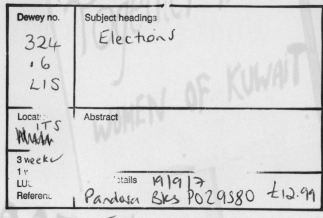

First published in 2006 by Franklin Watts
338 Euston Road, London NW1 3BH

Franklin Watts Australia
Hachette Children's Books
Level 17/207 Kent Street
Sydney NSW 2000

Series editor: Adrian Cole
Design: Thomas Keenes
Art director: Jonathan Hair
Picture researcher: Sarah Smithies

A CIP catalogue record for this book is
available from the British Library.

ISBN-10: 0 7496 6395 2
ISBN-13: 978 0 7496 6395 7

Dewey Classification: 324

Printed in China

Franklin Watts is a division of Hachette Children's Books.

Acknowledgements:
David Bathgate, Corbis: 16. David Davies, Empics: 18, 32.
Langevin Jacques, Corbis: 14. JLP/Deimos, Corbis: 23.
Brooks Kraft, Corbis: 9. LWA-Dann Tardif, Corbis: 21, 29.
LWA-Stephen Welstead, Corbis: 8, 22, 28 (fl), 28 (cl).
Dylan Martinez/Reuters, Corbis: 6 (r), 19, 30. Ahmad
Masood, Corbis: 17. Kathy McLaughlin, Topfoto: 6 (l), 25.
Newspix, Getty Images: 11. O'Brien Productions, Corbis:
24, 31. Chryssa Panoussiadou, Panos Pictures: cover and
7. Andrew Paterson, Alamy: 6 (c), 20. Michael Prince,
Corbis: 10, 28 (l). Paul A. Souders, Corbis: 27. David
Turnley, Corbis: 2, 13. Peter Turnley, Corbis: 12. Penny
Tweedie, Corbis: 4-5, 15. WorldFoto, Alamy: 26.

Contents

So what?

Most of the world's politicians are in power because people voted for them in an election. They know that if they don't do a good job, new politicians will be elected in their place at the next election.

What's it all about?

Elections and voting are part of a system of government called democracy. People are governed by representatives who they have chosen to lead them. But not everyone has the opportunity to choose their leaders, and even when they do, they don't always bother. On the following pages you will hear from a selection of people with different opinions about elections and voting, including a South African woman who never thought she would have the opportunity to vote, a young woman who lives in a country where only men can stand for election, and a sixteen-year-old who thinks she should be allowed to vote in elections.

Personal accounts

All of the testimonies are true. Some are first-hand accounts, while others are the result of bringing similar experiences together to create a single "voice". Every effort has been made to ensure they are authentic, but models have posed for some of the pictures. Wherever possible, permission to use the information has been obtained.

Ask yourself

The testimonies won't tell you all there is to know about elections and voting; that wouldn't be possible. Instead, as you encounter the different views, think about your own opinions. This will help you begin to address the question: "Elections and voting – what's that got to do with me?"

A man casts his vote by marking a ballot paper and posting it into a ballot box.

Choosing to vote

Not everyone has the chance to vote, but even when they do, some people choose not to. These are the voices of two very different voters. Tony has never voted – he doesn't see the point. Hilary always votes – she believes that her vote makes a difference.

Tony, a non-voter

I get up in the morning, take the kids to school and go to work. Sometimes, in the evening, I might go to a bar and play some pool with my friends. At the weekend we usually have a family trip, and occasionally we go away on holiday. That's my life. Now you tell me what do politicians have to do with any of that? They can talk about what they think is important as much as they like – but I won't listen. As far as I am concerned, all that money spent on elections would be better used to build more hospitals and schools.

For some people, elections have no place in their busy lives.

Fact bank

■ Countries where people vote for their governments are called democracies.

■ There are more democratic countries in the world now than ever before.

■ People become eligible to vote in the USA at 18. Less than a third of these voted in the 2004 US Presidential Elections.

President George W. Bush and First Lady Laura Bush celebrate an election victory.

Hilary, a voter

Democracy is such a precious thing and we're so lucky to have it. "We the people" have the chance to choose our leaders. That means politicians know if they don't do a good job, then they're out! There are many people in the world who can only dream of having such power. In those countries it's the people who serve the government, but where I live it's the members of the government who are the servants, because every few years they are answerable to us. Besides, if you don't vote, then how can you complain if you don't get the government you want?

Ask yourself this...

■ How would you describe Tony's attitude towards politics and politicians?

■ In which ways does politics affect your life? Who do you think makes decisions about hospitals and schools?

■ If democracy is "such a precious thing", as Hilary says, why do you think so many people who have the chance to vote in elections choose not to?

An advertiser

Stanley works for an advertising agency. He produces campaign material for political parties at election time. Over recent years, he has been working on more and more "negative campaigns" to help win them votes.

Very few voters can be bothered to read policies or manifestos, and those who do don't really believe them. The fact is, most people vote for the person they like the best. My job is quite straightforward – either to reflect "my client" politician in a most positive way or to create a really negative image for their opponent. It's much easier to get voters to believe negative things about politicians, so most of our time is spent convincing people not to vote for the other parties. We come up with catchy slogans, create cartoon figures, and do anything we can – within the law, of course. We never actually lie; we just play with the truth.

Many people don't like negative campaigns, but if you ask me, it lightens the mood a bit. Most politicians take themselves far too seriously and try to make us trust them by pretending to be completely squeaky-clean.

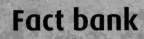
Advertisers help to win votes for politicians.

Fact bank

■ Negative campaigning is also called "attack" campaigning. It was first seen in the USA and its popularity has spread to many other countries, including Australia, New Zealand and the UK.

Medicare. Education. Jobs.

He lies. You pay.

VICTORIAN TRADES HALL COUNCIL

Lygon & Victoria Streets, Carlton South, Vic. 3053.
Road, North Melbourne, Vic. 3051

Books

A comedian unveils a negative advertisement about the Australian Prime Minister.

No one really believes they are, that's why negative campaigns are so effective. They really grab the attention of the voter in a short space of time, and persuade people who have not yet made up their mind who not to vote for.

■ Broadcasting standards in many countries restrict the content of election advertising campaigns to prevent them becoming personal attacks on an individual candidate.

■ In 2004, the top two political parties in the UK spent a total of £12 million on their advertising campaigns. In 2004, during the US election advertising campaign, George W. Bush spent in excess of £71 million on advertising.

Ask yourself this...

■ Why do you think politicians hire people like Stanley to help win them votes in an election?

■ How much do you agree that a politician's image is more important than their party's policies?

■ How important is it that voters trust the people they are voting for?

A South African voter

On 26 April 1994, after years of non-representation, black South Africans, like Maria, were allowed to vote in an election for the first time. Here, she remembers how she felt on that day.

I had been waiting for this day all my life. It was a great moment. All night I could not sleep, so I went to the polling station when it was still dark. It was freezing cold still but it did not matter. Many others were there already. Some had walked for miles – a lady next to me had pushed her mother in a wheelchair for a day to get there. It was unbelievable. It was freedom. As the sun came up we started to sing songs and hymns – "Thank Ye Lord for

Black people in South Africa queued for hours to cast their first vote.

What You Have Given Us" was the most popular. And we were all dressed in our finest clothes.

This was a dream come true – finally three and a half centuries of oppression was ending. I cried as I put my paper into the ballot box and spoke my son's name – Stevie. He was just one of the many thousands who had died in the struggle to bring about such a day.

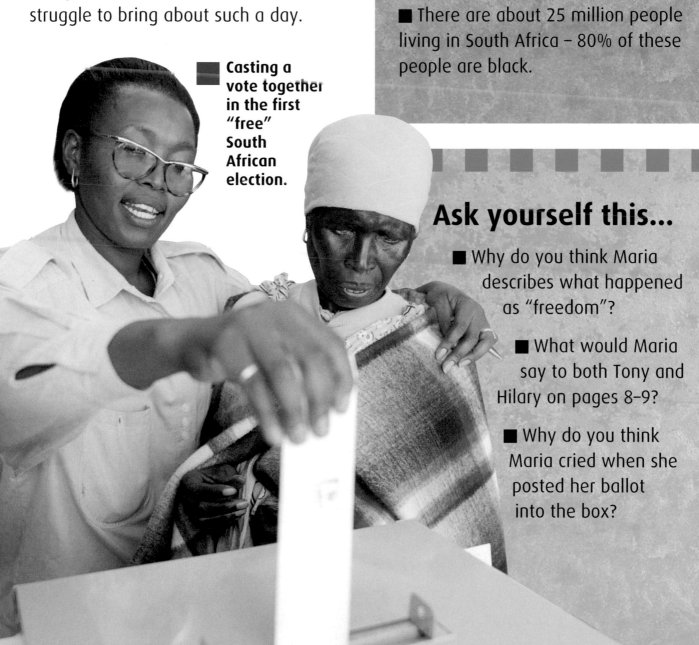

Casting a vote together in the first "free" South African election.

Fact bank

■ The first multi-racial elections in South Africa took place in 1994.

■ 85% of registered voters turned out for the 1994 election.

■ Until 1994, due to Apartheid, only white people were allowed to vote in parliamentary elections.

■ There are about 25 million people living in South Africa – 80% of these people are black.

Ask yourself this...

■ Why do you think Maria describes what happened as "freedom"?

■ What would Maria say to both Tony and Hilary on pages 8–9?

■ Why do you think Maria cried when she posted her ballot into the box?

A female voter

Farah is 12 and lives in Kuwait. Until 2005, women in her country were not allowed to take part in elections. Her mother has campaigned for women's rights, and now things are starting to improve in Kuwait.

My mother works for the government as a translator. She travels all over the world helping politicians who can't speak English, but she has never been allowed to vote for them in elections, until this year. She wants to become a Member of Parliament (MP) too, but women are not allowed to do that yet in my country. It is just not fair.

Fact bank

■ In 2005 the Kuwaiti parliament finally agreed that women should be allowed to vote.

■ Women in Australia won full political rights in 1902, in the USA it was 1920, but women in the UK had to wait until 1928.

■ Women are still not allowed to vote in Brunei, Saudi Arabia or the United Arab Emirates.

Now, when Farah is an adult, she will have the chance to vote in Kuwaiti elections.

Women across Kuwait have campaigned for equal political rights for many years.

Last year I went with her on a march to promote women's rights. Most of us wore light-blue clothes, the colour of women's rights in Kuwait. We held placards that said: "Equal rights now" and "Islamic law is not against women's rights". There were a lot of police there as well to protect us, because there are many people who opposed us. The government had been talking about changing the law, but I didn't think it would actually happen. But my mother says that change is inevitable.

Ask yourself this...

■ Why do you think some men want to prevent women from voting?

■ How important is it that every adult has the chance to vote?

■ Why do you think Farah's mother and her friends had to protest on the streets?

An Afghan actor

Until recently, people in Afghanistan were not allowed to take part in elections. This is the voice of an actor in Afghanistan who is helping people to understand how to vote, now the people are free to do so.

I am an actor. Most people in my country, Afghanistan, have never had the chance to choose who would lead us. Up until now it has been the ones with the most guns who have power – then we were given democracy. Now, we all have a chance to vote in an election. But almost no-one knew what that was – especially those living in the countryside where there is no television and most people can't read.

So my theatre company wrote a play to try to explain about "voting" and we toured as many villages as we could.

Voters reading newspapers in Afghanistan.

Fact bank

■ Afghanistan is a large, mostly rural country, made up of many ethnic groups. Elections took place there after the strict Taliban government was overthrown.

■ In 2004, 8 million people voted for a president in Afghanistan.

■ A year later, the first Assembly Elections for over 30 years took place, but the turnout was lower because of the confusingly large number of candidates, and the threat of attacks on voters in some areas.

■ Free radios were distributed to help spread information about the elections.

We showed them that our new leaders could only rule if we say they can. At first they didn't trust us, they thought that we were only joking. But when they realised we were serious, they were overjoyed.

Advertising in Afghanistan, as in many countries, encourages people to vote.

Ask yourself this...

■ Why do you think the villagers didn't trust the actors at first?

■ Some people were not happy about the introduction of democracy. What could be done to prevent their threats of violence keeping some voters away from the polling stations?

■ What are the benefits of a democratically elected government? Can you think of any disadvantages with this type of political system?

An independent politician

Stuart stood for election in Hartlepool, UK, as a joke. He didn't belong to a political party, he stood as an independent candidate. In the end he ended up being voted mayor – twice!

My job used to be to dress up as H'Angus – my football team's monkey mascot. I only stood for mayor to get the team more publicity. I didn't expect to win the town election, but when I did, I thought "what an honour", so I decided to give it my best shot.

I had to learn a lot very quickly. I got lots of support, because I wasn't linked to any of the political parties. People seemed more willing to trust me – especially when I got other politicians to work together. It worked – crime in the town has fallen by 20% since I took office, and everyone agrees that education is steadily improving and social services are doing well. After three years in the job, I was re-elected – it seems voters quite like independent politicians. And I didn't really campaign – my only leaflet promised the voters that I wouldn't flood their letterboxes or come knocking on their door, intruding on their privacy.

Stuart in his mascot outfit. He stood as an independent candidate in a local election.

Counting election ballots. Close results, like Stuart's first election, can lead to a recount.

Fact bank

■ People like Stuart, who don't belong to political parties, are called independent candidates.

■ All candidates have to pay a deposit of money before they can stand in elections.

■ Stuart won his first election by only 603 votes. Three years later he won the election again, but this time by 10,200 votes.

Ask yourself this...

■ What is the appeal of an independent candidate?

■ Why did Stuart's attitude change after he was elected?

■ Why do you think candidates have to pay a deposit before they can stand for election?

■ What lessons could the main political parties learn from Stuart's success?

A young voter

In many countries you have to be 18 years old to vote, but some people think that's not young enough. Jiang Li is 14 years old and from the USA. She feels that young teenagers deserve more respect.

I'm fed up with being treated like a kid – especially when some of those so-called "grown-up" politicians behave so badly. I don't think physical age has anything to do with when you should be allowed to vote.

Why do you have to be 18 years old before you have a say in how your country is run? Everyone is affected by pollution from industries that the

Fact bank

■ 16-year-olds can legally marry, join the army and pay taxes to the government.

■ In the UK it is possible to hold a pilot's and driving licence at 17.

■ In 1972, the voting age in US Presidential Elections was reduced from 21 to 18. Since then, fewer and fewer potential first-time voters have actually cast their vote.

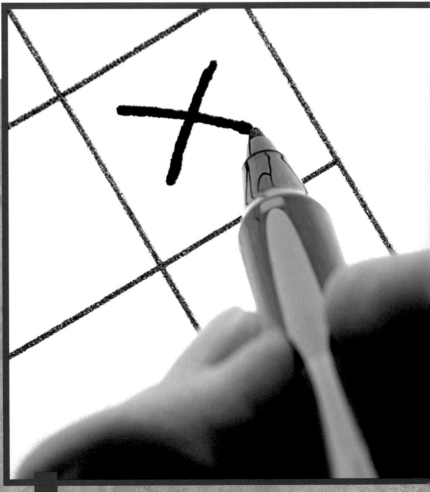

People vote by placing an "X" next to the name of their selected candidate.

government controls. You don't have to be 18 to live in poverty in one of the richest countries in the world. We walk the same streets as adults, use the same public healthcare programmes as them, and of course, we have to attend the under-funded schools that they don't need to worry about now. By the time we get to have our say, it's too late!

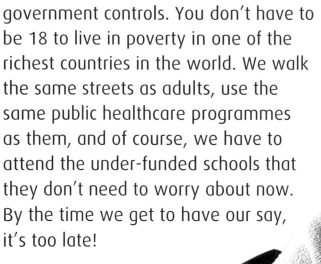

Many young teenagers want to have more of a say through voting.

Ask yourself this...

■ At what age do you think people should be allowed to vote?

■ What other ways are there for people to play a part in making things better, other than through voting?

■ Why do you think there is a minimum voting age?

21

A TV voter

Although Jodie is only 10 years old, she has voted more times than her parents. Television and Internet voting have become popular ways to encourage the audience to take part in what is happening on screen.

My mum and dad had to wait until they were 18 to vote. I'm 10, and I can do it as much as I like. I vote for my favourite singer on TV programmes, like Pop Idol. You don't have to go out to vote like you do in an election. I can phone, text or press the red button on my remote, without even getting up. I think if it was this easy to vote in political elections, many more people would do it.

I have to ask Mum or Dad for permission before I vote on the TV – but they are pleased when I ask. Dad says it gets me used to the idea of "exercising my democratic right". And there are lots of polls on the Internet: favourite pop-song, best outfit, most good-looking film star. All you have to do is click the mouse to take part.

■ Telephone voting is just one of many ways to vote during some TV programmes.

Fact bank

■ More British 18–34-year-olds voted on the 2005 final of Big Brother than voted in the 2005 General Election.

■ In political elections some people post their vote, but most people still visit a polling station.

■ You can only vote once in a political election. Television viewers can vote as many times as they like.

■ Many countries are considering the introduction of Internet and text voting for political elections.

Internet voting is extremely popular amongst children aged 8–16.

Ask yourself this...

■ How important is it to make it easier for people to vote?

■ Why do you think so many people vote during TV programmes?

■ What is the difference between voting on the Internet for your favourite pop star, and voting for a political party during an election?

A school council candidate

Nathan is standing for a place on the school student council. He has to persuade people to vote for him by campaigning, just like adult politicians.

I really want to serve on the student council because I want to help improve things, like school meals and the school football pitch. I also want to stop the bullying at school. But before I can do that I have to win an election. Each class votes for their representative, and

Fact bank

■ Many schools have student councils where young people can give their opinions, and sometimes influence aspects of school life.

■ During General and Presidential Elections, many schools copy the voting process by organising their own versions.

■ 1.5 million US children voted in an on-line "mock" Presidential Election.

Young people can become involved in politics at their school.

Starting a student council campaign. These students are designing a campaign poster.

there are three candidates from my class. That means I have to convince everyone else I am the best choice. The teachers have allowed us to make only one poster each and, unlike in real elections, we mustn't say anything against our opponents. The class candidates have to make a three-minute speech to the class. I just practised it in front of my mum. She said that I should buy everyone some sweets to get them to vote for me.

Ask yourself this...

■ What good do you think school student councils can do?

■ If your school has a student council, what issues does it discuss?

■ What would you change if you were a school student councillor?

■ Why do you think the teachers allowed the candidates to make only one poster, and prevented them from saying negative things?

■ Why did Nathan's mum suggest buying sweets for everyone?

Compulsory voting

By law, all people resident in Australia must vote in political elections. Dennis is an Australian and would vote anyway, but he thinks the law should be changed.

I don't want to sound big headed, but I'm a pretty smart bloke. I speak three languages, went to university and I run my own business. I have a big interest in politics and I study all the election material before I vote. I read as much as I can, and I don't decide where my vote's going until the night before election day. But when I vote I find myself queuing with people who don't really understand what they're doing. They just don't want to be fined for not turning up. I bet they don't give their vote more than five minutes' thought, yet they have as much influence on the outcome of the election as me. Well, that's just wrong. Who cares if those who are uninterested and unintelligent don't vote? The country would be much better served if only those who really understood politics were allowed to vote, and everyone else just accepted the result that the more able and informed decide.

Some Australians don't believe in forcing people to vote.

People in Sydney, Australia. Everyone has to vote in political elections.

Fact bank

■ Voting has been compulsory in Australia since 1924.

■ Compulsory voting is designed to increase participation in elections.

■ Australians who don't vote could be fined or sent to prison.

■ On average about 95% of Australians register a vote. In the UK about 60% of people vote, and in the USA it's only 50%.

Ask yourself this...

■ How would you describe Dennis' views?

■ How important is it that as many people as possible vote during an election?

■ What would those voters who don't spend as much time studying politics say about Dennis' ideas? Should they be given a choice not to vote if they don't want to?

What do elections and voting have to do with me?

Elections are a chance for whole populations to have their say. Voting is all about making your opinion count. Losing politicians accept the result because they know that the outcome is the choice of the people. Today there are more countries in the world that choose their governments by voting than there have ever been. But, as we have seen in this book, not everyone agrees with the way elections work. As a British Prime Minister, Winston Churchill, once said: "Democracy is the worst form of government except for all those others that have been tried."

To help you form your own opinion about elections and voting, and to find out the opinions of others, with your parent or teacher, copy out the questionnaire opposite. Then give the questions to your friends and ask them to consider all the statements carefully before making a decision. They can "vote" by saying whether they agree or disagree with each one. Finally, collect all the questionnaires together and add up the results to see what your friends think that elections and voting have to do with them.

Elections and voting questionnaire

1. You should always use your vote, even if you do not want to vote for any of the politicians or parties.
Agree / Disagree.

2. All politicians are the same, they never tell the truth.
Agree / Disagree.

3. Negative campaigning should be banned. People should only be allowed to promote their own political party.
Agree /
Disagree.

4. You should be able to text-vote in political elections.
Agree /
Disagree.

5. Voting is a waste of time. It never makes any difference.
Agree / Disagree.

6. Independent politicians are not as effective in government when compared to politicians who belong to a political party.
Agree / Disagree.

7. The current voting age should be reduced so people aged 16 have the right to vote.
Agree / Disagree.

8. Everyone, including refugees and prisoners, should be allowed to vote.
Agree / Disagree.

9. Schools are no place for elections.
Agree / Disagree.

10. Everybody should be made to vote by law.
Agree /
Disagree.

Websites

The websites below feature more information, news articles and stories that you can use to help form your own opinions. Use the information carefully and consider the source it comes from before drawing any conclusions.

www.australianpolitics.com
A comprehensive website featuring information about the Australian parliament, constitution, voting system and election procedures.

www.youthrights.org/ votingage.shtml
US-based website of the National Youth Rights Association, featuring articles, discussion points and an action newsletter.

www.parliament.govt.nz/ politics-news.html
Find out more about the political parties in New Zealand on this House of Representatives website.

www.electoralcommission. org.uk
Find out more about elections and voting on this website from the UK Electoral Commission.

www.number-10.gov.uk
Website of the historic home of the British Prime Minister, featuring up-to-date political news and a guided tour.

www.peo.gov.au
This Australian Parliamentary Education Office website includes resources and news.

www.schoolcouncils.org
Information about how to set up, structure and improve school councils.

Glossary

Apartheid – government policy in South Africa that made the separation of different races legal.

Ballot box – the official box in which folded ballot papers are placed. They are emptied later and the votes counted.

Ballot paper – a special voting slip, with a list of candidates' names on and a space to mark an "X".

Campaign – a number of different events, including advertisements, public appearances and speeches, designed to encourage people to vote for one political party.

Candidate – a person standing for election to a government or other democratic body, including a school student council.

Cast – to vote.

Democracy – a political system in which members of government are elected by the votes of the general population.

Ethnic – sharing the same cultural and racial identity.

General Election – the main election held in the UK when a political party is elected to run the government.

Manifesto – the collection of policies produced by a political party: the party manifesto.

Non-representation – the situation that occurs when a group of people in a community are excluded from a public event, such as an election or debate.

Policy – a group of aims produced by a political party.

Polling station – a public building taken over during an election so that people can cast their vote. It has private booths so that people can keep their vote secret.

Taliban – the strict Islamic, tribal-based government that controlled Afghanistan prior to its invasion.

Women's rights – equal rights in pay, social status and other freedoms for women, especially when compared to those held by men.

Index